# I Want A Leopard Gecko

## 2020 Edition

Tristan Pulsifer and

Jacquelyn Elnor Johnson

Crimson Hill
Books

www.CrimsonHillBooks.com

First edition, October 2016.

Revised, January 2020.

**Cataloguing in Publication Data**

Pulsifer, Tristan | Johnson, Jacquelyn Elnor

I Want A Leopard Gecko | Best Pets For Kids Series

Description: Crimson Hill Books trade paperback edition | Nova Scotia, Canada

ISBN 978-0-9953191-2-7 (Paperback)

BISAC: JNF003190 Juvenile Nonfiction: Animals - Reptiles & Amphibians
JNF003170 Juvenile Nonfiction: Animals – Pets
JNF051150 Juvenile Nonfiction: Science & Nature – Zoology

THEMA: YNNM - Children's / Teenage general interest: Reptiles & amphibians |
YNNH - Children's / Teenage general interest: Pets & pet care

Record available at https://www.bac-lac.gc.ca/eng/Pages/home.aspx

Cover Photo: Jan Pietruszka, Stockfresh.com
Book design: Jesse Johnson

We are pet owners, not veterinarians. Nothing included in this book is meant to serve as medical advice. If you suspect your pet is ill, please see your local vet. We accept no liability concerning your pet ownership.

Crimson Hill Books
(a division of)
Crimson Hill Products Inc.
Wolfville, Nova Scotia
Canada

# Contents

# What Every Pet Leopard Gecko Needs

It's so exciting to think about getting your new pet, isn't it?

But before you do, you need to know what they will need. Are you sure you can give your leopard gecko all these things, to keep them healthy and happy?

1. A tank or enclosure for their new home that is big enough for them.

2. A heater. Usually this is a basking light that hangs above their tank, at one end.

3. Light tubes that are as long as the tank is. They also hang at the top.

4. You'll need thermometers, to be sure it is always warm enough for your pet, everywhere in their tank. Or cool enough.

5. Three hides. These are places they go to rest or sleep.

6. A water bowl, big enough to drink out of or take a dip!

7. A food dish.

8. The right substrate. This is what goes on the floor of their new home.

9. Calcium and vitamins they need to stay strong and have a long healthy life. These are called supplements.

10. Live insects and insect worms. That's all leopard geckos eat! Find out which kinds in this book.

11. Regular feeding, attention and care.

**Find out more about all of these leo needs in this book!**

# **Introduction**

# **What is a Leopard Gecko?**

*This is a pet leopard gecko.*

## **What is a gecko?**

Geckos are one type of lizard.

All lizards are reptiles.

The reptile family includes turtles, alligators, crocodiles, snakes, birds and tuataras [here's how to

*This is a wild tuatara.*

say it: TOO-a-tare-ah]. Most wild reptiles live in many parts of the world, but tuataras are very rare. They live only in New Zealand.

Leopard geckos and tuataras look very different from each other. But they both have two things that every reptile has:

**1.** scales that cover at least part of their bodies,
**2.** they are cold-blooded (except for birds)

Cold-blooded means when they are too cold, they don't have any way to warm up their bodies.

When they're too hot, they don't sweat to cool off.

To get warm, cold-blooded creatures must find some heat, like going to sit in the sun.

When they are too hot, they have to find a cooler place.

If they can't do this, they will get very sick and might die.

Most of the world's creatures are cold-blooded. Only birds and mammals are warm-blooded.

Warm-blooded means they are able to make their own body heat. Horses, dogs, mice and people are all mammals.

Most reptiles do not make good pets. They want to live alone and be wild animals.

There are some reptiles that make great pets. One of the best for kids or new pet owners of any age is the leopard gecko.

## Is a gecko like a snake?

Geckos and snakes are alike in some ways.

Both are reptiles.

Both live as wild animals or can be tamed as pets (though there are some types of lizards and also some types of snakes that make very bad pets!).

Both geckos and snakes have heads that are triangle-shaped.

Both shed their skins.

Both leopard geckos and some types of snakes have sharp teeth, but they can't chew their food. They have to swallow it whole.

*This is a pet corn snake. Photo: Cynoclub, Stockfresh.*

*This little guy is a wild fire belly newt. Some newts look like small geckos, but all newts are amphibians.*

Snakes can't close their eyes, but geckos can. Snakes don't have ears, but geckos do.

In times of danger, a gecko's tail falls off so it can escape. No snake can do this. A really amazing thing is that when a gecko's tail breaks off, it will quickly grow back. The new tail will be different then their old tail. It might be short and stubby. Or a bit crooked.

Both snakes and geckos have a super sense of smell. Leopard geckos also have keen eyesight.

## Is a gecko an amphibian?

No, amphibians are a different family group than reptiles.

The amphibian family includes frogs, toads and salamanders.

Some amphibians might look a little like reptiles, but this is why they are different:

Amphibians have smooth, moist skin that is sometimes sticky. Reptiles have dry skin with scales.

Both amphibians and reptiles can have legs and feet, but only lizards have claws.

Both hatch from eggs. The babies never know their parents.

A big difference is that amphibians mostly live in water. They lay their eggs in water.

Reptiles mostly live on land. They have to lay their eggs on land.

## Where do geckos come from?

Wild geckos were first discovered in Asia, throughout Pakistan and in northern and western India.

Wild geckos do not make good pets.

*This is a wild tokay gecko at a nature reserve in Thailand.*

Today, leopard geckos are captive bred to be pets. Captive bred means they and their parents and grandparents were born and raised as pets.

They were never wild. Most leo pets today come from ancestors who were wild leos in Pakistan.

## Wild Leos

Where would you go to find wild leopard geckos? The answer is the rocky and dry grasslands and deserts of Afghanistan, Pakistan, Iran or north-west India.

Though usually hot and dry, these places can get cold in winter. The temperature can dip to lower than 50 degrees F. (10 degrees C.) When it gets cold, wild geckos go to sleep in underground burrows.

For lizards, this kind of hibernating is called brumation. (Here's how to say it: BREW–may-shun). It is a lot like hibernation. That's a long winter snooze when they might want to eat less and are less active.

During brumation, they stay alive because of the fat stored in their tails. When it warms up again outside, they wake up and come back to the surface.

## How are wild geckos different from pet geckos?

Wild leopard geckos aren't as brightly-coloured as pet geckos. They are always yellowish and brown, with spots.

They are far more timid. They try to avoid humans and live most of their lives alone.

## What makes leopard geckos different from other geckos?

Leopard geckos have brown spots on their backs and tails that look like a leopard's coat.

Unlike most other lizards, leos have eyelids. They can wink at you!

Leopard geckos have smooth, cool skin. There are bumps on their backs and their bellies are dry and smooth.

### *Leo Fact: Big Family*

*There are at least 1,500 types of geckos in the world today. Only a few types are happy to be pets.*

*This juvenile leopard gecko is 3 months old.*

*Shedding leos need gentle help. Don't pull off the dead skin. Photo: Tim Jasinski, Flickr.com.*

### *Leo Fact: Leos can bark!*

*Most reptiles (except birds) are mostly silent. Not leos!*

*They can call, chirp and bark to let others know where they are.*

*Pet leos don't often do this but they do squeal when threatened or afraid. They make a squeaky hiss when surprised.*

# Chapter One

# Why can a Leopard Gecko be a Good Pet?

There are many types of geckos. Only some make good pets.

Leos are the best gecko to choose as a pet because they are more gentle, quiet and well-behaved than any other type of gecko.

They look interesting. There are lots of different colours and patterns.

Leos are sweet, friendly and easy to care for and keep healthy. They always seem to be smiling.

Also, they don't get very big. They don't need a lot of space for their home.

Leopard geckos don't need a lot of attention, because they are happy to be alone. You won't need to brush their coat or take them for walks. They will never chew on the furniture or break things.

Leos can live in a small space and are easy to feed.

Even though geckos are a small creature, they are fun to have. They will climb up in your hand to say hello. They're a friendly creature.

They could bite when they are very upset. If they do, you will hardly feel it.

*This is a juvenile leo. Juvenile means not still a baby, but not an adult yet. Photo: Fouroaks, Stockfresh.com*

Unlike bearded dragons, you can have one or two leos in the same vivarium or tank as some other lizard pets, such as these: Amarillo lizards, Collared lizards, South African flat lizards and small Girdle-tailed lizards. Some of these lizards must have a UV (ultra-violet) light above the tank.

## Who would NOT enjoy having a gecko and why?

If you want a pet you can run around and play with outside, the pet for you is a dog. Geckos are an indoor pet. If your family travels a lot, will there be someone back home to care for your gecko? Leos don't enjoy travelling.

It is not a good idea to have any type of reptile pet if there is a baby or child who is younger than age 5 in your family. It wouldn't be safe for the baby or young child, or for your gecko.

To own any pet, you need to be responsible.

Your pet is depending on you for food and everything else he or she needs.

Do you think you will give your gecko good care, even when you don't really feel like it?

Leopard geckos are crepuscular [here's how to say it: cray-pus-cue-lar].

This means they are most active just after sunrise. This would be about when you're waking up in the morning.

Their other active time is just before sunset, or late afternoon or evening for humans.

If you want a pet that is active during the daytime, a leopard gecko might not be the right pet for you.

Leopard geckos can live a really long time.

If you are age 10 now, your pet leo could still be alive when you are 20, or even when you are 25.

Are you sure you will always want this pet and will be happy to look after him or her for a long time?

### Leo Fact: Get some bugs!

*Leopard geckos eat live insects. They want to chase their food. If you get a gecko, you'll also need to care for the insects they eat!*

# 10 Reasons Why Leos Make Great Pets

What are the advantages of having a pet leopard gecko?

1. Little leos don't need a lot of attention, like some other kinds of pets. They're content to spend time alone in their tank, just as long as they get some playtime with you each day.

2. They don't need to be groomed.

3. You never need to take them for walks.

4. They live in a smaller space than most other pets. Even a small bedroom has enough room for a leo's tank!

5. They're easy to feed.

6. They won't ever chew on your slippers or destroy your house.

7. They're a quiet pet.

8. They aren't smelly if you keep their tank clean.

9. They're easy to keep healthy. You will hardly ever have to take them to the vet.

10. They live longer than most other types of pets. They can be your friend for a long time to come!

# <u>Chapter Two</u>

# Questions and Answers About Pet Leopard Geckos

## How long do they live?

Leopard geckos that are pets usually live about eight to ten years. But some leos live as long as 20 years or more.

Males usually live longer than females. The oldest known pet leo lives at a zoo. He is more than 30 years old!

## How big do they get?

A hatchling is a baby that just came out of their egg. They are about 3 inches (9 cm) long.

Adults are about 8 inches (20.3 cm) long. Males are usually a bit bigger than females. Some giant leopard geckos can grow up to 12 inches (30 cm) long.

## Do leos change colour? What colours do they come in?

Baby leos do change colour. They don't look the same as adults. They don't get the spotted pattern on their backs and tails until they are older.

*When babies are about 4 months old and 4 inches (10 cm) long, they can be adopted. Photo: Doug Pulsifer.*

Leos usually have a background colour of gray, yellow or orangey-yellow. They don't get their brown spots until they are adults.

Fancy leos are called morphs. They can be orange, reddish orange or almost white. They might also have stripes.

## Do leos like to be handled?

Most do after they get to know you, especially during their active times of day.

If a leopard gecko squeals or makes a hissing sound, it means you are not being gentle enough. Or it wants to be left alone right now.

You also have to protect leos from falling to the floor.

Remember to be gentle with them!

*Playing with a juvenile leo. Photo: J. E. Johnson.*

## Are geckos active?

Leopard geckos aren't very active during the day or at night. If they live in your bedroom, they won't wake you up at night!

The time when your gecko wants to see you, be active and eat is early in the morning or in the evening, during twilight. Twilight is the time when the sun is setting.

## Are leopard geckos smelly?

No, they are a very clean animal. They always poop in just one corner of their tank. This makes it easy to scoop the poop every day and keep them un-stinky.

## Can leos wag their tails?

Baby geckos can get so excited about being fed that they will wag the tip of their tails. Adults don't do this.

## Are they poisonous?

No, but it is very important to always wash your hands with warm water and soap before AND after you touch a gecko. Just using hand sanitizer is not enough.

There is a very small chance that you could catch an illness from a gecko – or it could catch an illness from you.

*This baby leo is shedding. Photo: Debbie Pulsifer.*

## Do they shed their skin?

Yes, baby leos shed their skin almost every week. Adult leos shed their skin about once a month. Then they eat the skin. No one knows exactly why they do this. But it is very interesting to watch!

You will know your leo is getting ready to shed when his or her skin starts to look gray-ish. After shedding, a leo's coat is brightly-coloured again.

## Is a leopard gecko a leapin' lizard?

Yes!

Geckos are curious creatures. They can move really quickly, especially baby geckos.

Sometimes they will try to leap out of your hands if you aren't careful.

If they do get loose in your home, it could be very hard to catch them again!

## Can geckos see in the dark?

No creature can see when it is totally dark. But many animals can see better than people can when there isn't very much light.

In low-light conditions, people see everything as shades of gray. This means everything looks like it is lighter gray, or darker gray. We can't see in color when it's almost dark, but many animals can, including geckos.

Leopard geckos see blues and grays, and possibly also greens in low light. They probably can't see red.

## How much time does it take to care for a pet gecko?

Leos take less time to care for than just about any other pet.

Feeding them takes just a few minutes every day (for baby leos).

Adults should only be fed two or three times a week.

All leos need fresh water everyday.

You need to clean the poop in their tank often – once a day is good. This just takes a minute or two.

Their tank needs to be cleaned once a week. It could take 15 minutes or so. Clean with soapy water with a bit of bleach in it. Rinse thoroughly before your leo goes back into their freshly-cleaned home.

You also need to take care of your crickets and worms. This takes just a few minutes every day.

## How much help will I need from my parents (or someone older)?

You will need some help setting up the tank and getting used to caring for your leo.

Someone older will need to drive you to the pet store to buy more crickets and feeder worms. You could also buy them online.

You might need help setting up a Feeding Routine and Care Routine for your new pet.

*An adult pet leo in a nicely setup vivarium.*

## When to Go to The Vet

Take your leo to the vet or a reptile expert right away if:

- They are twitching or bleeding. This might be serious, or they may just need more supplements.
- They have lost weight in their tail.
- They won't eat and have no energy.

These problems are not as serious, but you might still need help if your leo has diarrhea, is constipated, or a toe or the tip of their tail turns brown or black. This can happen when old skin doesn't completely shed.

*This adult leo is warming himself under a heat lamp on a nice, comfortable rock.*

### Leo Tip: Warning! Danger!

*Never let your pet eat these. They could make them very sick or even kill a leo!*

- *Any wild insect or worm from outside*
- *Monarch butterflies*
- *Ladybugs*
- *Spiders*
- *Centipedes*

# Chapter Three

# How to Get Your Gecko

There are many ways to get a gecko.

Pet stores are a place to find your pet gecko. Or you could look online for a quality gecko breeder. Or go to a herp show, where you will see many geckos offered for sale.

A herp show is a big trade show for people who have reptile pets, or want one.

Herp shows, like the one the poster on the next page is advertising, happen about once a year, usually in big cities.

Herp is short for herpetology [say it like this: HER-pet-taw-low-gee] Herpetologists are the scientists who study amphibians and reptiles.

You may have to travel a long way to go to a herp show, but it is worth it. You will see hundreds of awesome reptiles there, including leos. You will also meet leopard gecko breeders. These shows are very popular!

Today, all leopard geckos are captive bred. They are not captured wild animals that are imported into our country (and could bring diseases with them).

This means geckos you can buy are born to be pets.

Good breeders (the people who sell baby geckos and other types of reptiles) only sell healthy animals.

# The Manitoba Reptile Breeder's Expo
## September 24th & 25th, 2016
### 10am - 5pm
### VIP Access 9am (Saturday Only)
### Weekend passes available
### Canad Inns Polo Park - Ambassador Rooms 1 & 2
### 1405 St Matthews Ave, Winnipeg

# Tickets $10.00
## Kids 12 and under FREE!

Tickets at the door - Info available online - Free parking

**Presented by: Winnipeg Reptiles & Prairie Exotics**

With top breeders from Winnipeg and across Manitoba!

**www.TheMRBE.com**

*This is a poster for a herp show. The little guy at the lower right is a leo.*

If you get tired of your pet, you cannot just let him or her go free in your back yard. This would be cruel, because they will not survive.

## How much do pet geckos cost?

Depending on where you live and where you buy your gecko, it could cost from about $20 to $80 for a leopard gecko.

You should know that there are some very exotic geckos that sell for as much as $3,000! They are expensive because of their rare colours and patterns.

## Who will pay for your leopard gecko?

One question parents always ask is, "But how much does it cost to have this pet? Who will pay for it?"

It's a good question because no pet is free to get or to have. Leos need two things that cost money. These are heat and food.

Heat comes from the heating pad or heat strips under the tank, or a better choice is a heat light over the tank. These run on electricity, but it is a very small amount. So your family's electricity bill will go up, but not by very much.

Leopard geckos eat crickets and insect worms. These could cost $15 or $20 per month.

Before you get your gecko, you need to know who will pay for him or her.

*A Red Spotted Enigma leo morph by RedGeckos, Flickr.com*

# How to get your Leo for Less Money

If you want a leo but need your new pet to cost less money, here are some ideas:

1. Pet stores sometimes put tanks on sale. Or you could save money by buying a used tank. Look for ads in community newspapers and on free online ad sites to find a good used tank. Another idea is to make a tank. It can open at the top or have front sliding doors, making it easy to clean. You'll need an adult to help you make a vivarium tank.

2. Most pet rescue shelters won't accept reptiles. But there are a few pet shelters that only take reptiles.

   Look to see if there is one near where you live. They may have a little leo looking for a good new home.

3. Sometimes pet owners find they can no longer keep their pets. Look in local newspapers and online at free ads to see if there is someone who wants a new home for their leo.

   Often they will sell their pet with the tank and everything that goes with it. Prices we've seen lately have been about $35 to $80 to adopt a leopard gecko from another pet owner, with the tank. But beware! Only adopt a healthy pet!

4. There are lots of ways to make hides that leos will love. Get creative!

5. You'll save money on crickets when you buy them online. They can cost even less when you raise your own instead of buying them.

## Should you get a baby gecko?

Baby geckos are so cute! But babies always need more time and care than adults.

For one thing, baby leos need to be fed more often than adults.

With good care, a baby gecko will become an adult before he or she is one year old.

## Should you buy two geckos so they have a friend in their tank?

Geckos are happy to live alone.

If you do decide to have two leos in the same tank, it should be two females. They should be about the same size and same age.

You can't put a male and female together unless you want the female to have babies.

And you can't put two males together because they will fight and could hurt each other.

## Which leo should I get?

Choose one that is in a clean enclosure and looks well cared for.

Your leo should have bright eyes and be alert and active with lots of energy.

His or her tail should be as rounded and wide as the body. Make sure they have all their fingers and toes.

*A healthy leo's eyes should be bright and clear.*

Try to be there when the gecko you want is being fed. A healthy gecko is a good eater.

You also want a friendly gecko, not one that squeals with fear when people get close. You don't want a scaredy-cat gecko!

Don't buy a skinny gecko or one that doesn't move very much because you feel sorry for it. A skinny gecko is a sick gecko that might not live very long.

### Leo Tip: Leo Food

*Little leos could choke on food that is too big for them to swallow!*

*The right size for your leo is an insect or worm shorter then the length of your pet's head.*

*Close up of leo scales and their beautiful eyes. Photo: Adam Browning, Flickr.com*

### Leo Tip: What about Cleaning?

*Leos don't need baths, but they do enjoy a water dish large enough to sit in!*

*Clean their tank and everything in it twice a month. Put your leo in a safe place. Empty their tank. Wash everything with warm soapy water mixed with 1 part bleach to 9 parts water. Rinse thoroughly!*

# Chapter Four

# Getting Ready for Your New Pet

*This little gecko looks like most of the leos you'll see at a pet store. Photo: Debbie Pulsifer.*

It's best to have everything you need to welcome your gecko to his or her new home before you get your gecko.

You need a tank that is set up just the way geckos like. You also need the food they like to eat.

### Leo Fact: Bright Colours!

*Leos that live alone tend to have brighter colours than when they live in a group. No-one knows why this strange fact is true!*

37

## What kind of food do geckos eat?

Live insects, insect worms and pinkie mice and nothing else. They will not eat fruit or vegetables.

Leopard geckos like crickets and insect worms like butterworms, hornworms and Phoenix worms.

You can get these at the pet store or online.

Geckos also need to take their vitamins! Buy reptile vitamins, calcium and D3 powder at the pet store (or online).

The D3 might be in with the vitamins, or it could be in with the calcium. It shouldn't be in both. There is a danger that your leo could get too much D3.

Vitamins, D3 and calcium for leopard geckos are not pills. They are a powder.

You put this powder all over an insect by gently shaking the insect and the powder together in a small bag.

Then feed the powdery insect to your gecko right away.

Your feeder insects need to eat too.

Feed your crickets or feeder worms with raw apple or carrot slices and raw oats.

If your gecko doesn't eat the insect or worm right away, take it out of the tank.

If you leave feeder crickets or worms in the tank and your gecko falls asleep, the insects could bite your gecko and injure him or her!

## What kind of tank will my leo need?

You need a tank for your gecko's new home. A 10 gallon (38 litre) tank is big enough to start with for one gecko. It is better for your leo if you get a bigger tank.

Geckos can't climb on a smooth surface like glass, so they won't escape from the tank.

There must be a screen lid on the gecko tank if you have other pets. A cat or dog might think your gecko looks good to eat!

You also need to set up their home so they can't get too close to the lights at the top and get burned.

## There are several things you need inside a leo's tank

Leos need some heat in their tank! This is because leos must have belly heat to digest their food.

They also need a way to cool off if they get too hot!

There are two easy ways to keep your leo warm enough:

1. You could have an under-pad heater that goes underneath part of the tank.
2. Or, for extra heat you could use a light hanging over just one part of the tank.

Using either an under-pad heater OR a light over one part of the tank will give your leo the heat she or he needs.

If you use a light, it needs to be on a timer to turn it off at night and on in the daytime.

Leos are very stressed by having a bright light on all the time. Just like you would be when you want to sleep.

## Leos love to have lots of places to climb up onto.

A climbing branch or pile of flat rocks is a good choice.

You can buy them at pet stores or online. Don't just use something you find outside, because it could have bugs or make your leo sick.

*This is a dry hide. Photo: D. Pulsifer.*

## Leos like to hide

Leos must have dark places to go to be alone and rest or sleep.

These places are called hides because they are where a gecko goes to hide.

You will need three hides in your new gecko's home.

1. One hide needs to be dry and in the warmest part of the tank.

**2.** Put another dry hide in the coolest part of the tank.

**3.** The third hide can be in the middle. It is just like the other two, except that it needs to be kept wet inside.

One way to keep your wet hide cool and moist is to put some paper towel inside the wet hide. Put water on the paper towel so that it is always damp.

*Rosie steps into her wet hide. The black cord in this photo is part of the tank thermometer. (A thermometer shows the temperature).*

You can buy fancy hides at the pet store.

Or you could make simple hides that your gecko will be just as happy with.

There are lots of ways to make a hide. You could use a broken plant pot, bowl or coconut shell. Just be sure there are no sharp edges that could hurt your gecko.

You could create a hide out of a pile of flat stones. Or just use a paper towel roll for the dry warm hide or dry cool hide.

A hide always needs to be big enough for your gecko to get in and out easily.

A upside-down plastic food container with a hole cut in the side makes a good wet hide. Check that the hole you cut on the side is big enough with smooth edges.

When you set up the tank, be sure that there are no places where your gecko could get stuck, like between a rock and the tank wall.

Another thing you will need is a water dish that is easy for your leo to get into.

Sometimes, geckos want a bath so they can cool off. The water needs to be just deep enough to cover your leo's belly.

Get a food dish that is easy for your gecko to grab crickets or worms out of. You could buy a reptile food dish, or use a shallow dish that your family already has.

Or you could feed your gecko one insect at a time and watch him or her eat it. This way, you won't need a food dish.

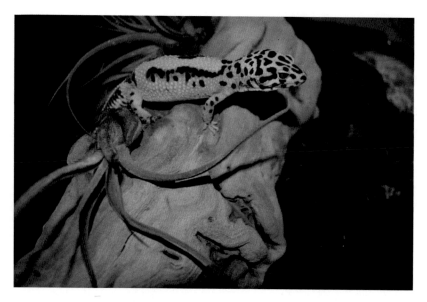

*A natural vivarium with aloe plants. Photo: Sohrob Tahmasebi, Pixabay.com*

Creating a natural looking tank is part of the fun of having a leo!

To make your tank more interesting, you could put in some plants in small pots. A gecko doesn't have to have plants in his or her tank, but they look good.

Leos really like to bask on a branch or a flat rock. Basking is when a lizard just hangs out in a warm place and takes a nap.

Leopard geckos can get bored with their tank and being in a small space.

Every three weeks or so, you should change around your tank's set-up. Moving the flat rocks, branches, hides and plants will keep life interesting for your gecko.

## Here are four things you <u>don't</u> need in your gecko's tank:

1. **You don't need sand in the bottom of the tank**. Geckos sometimes accidentally swallow the sand with their food. This can make them really sick. Paper towel, flat rocks, pea gravel, astro-turf (this is fake grass) or nothing at all on the floor of the tank is a safer choice for your young gecko. You can use play sand when they're an adult.

2. **You don't need a heated rock** from the pet store. This is a bad idea to have because it can get too hot and burn your pet.

3. **You don't need dried reptile food flakes**. Just about any leo will turn up his or her snout and refuse to eat it. They need their food to be alive.

4. **You don't need gecko toys**. Leos like lots of places to sit, climb, rest and hide. They don't care about toys.

## What makes the best floor for your leo's tank?

1. Reptile tile (you can buy this at most pet stores or online).

*Rearrange your leo's tank each week after you clean it. This keeps it interesting for your pet.*

**2.** Flat stone tiles
**3.** Astroturf or reptile carpet. Be sure to get the kind that your pet can't get their claws caught in. Wash it twice a month.
**4.** Paper towels or newspaper is best for babies and juveniles.

Never use these: Calcium sand. Wood shavings, because it is poison to geckos. Don't use gravel because it can damage their skin. Don't use anything that is dusty, because they will have breathing problems.

# Where to put your leo's tank

Put your leo's tank in a place where you can enjoy seeing your pet all the time.

In your bedroom is fine if your bedroom is always the right temperature for a gecko.

The tank needs to NOT be next to a heater, air conditioner, in a draft or direct sunlight. It's just too hot!

Leos also need no lights on at night.

Leos like a quiet life. Lots of loud noises will make your gecko sick.

If you like to make a lot of noise or need to practice playing the drums in your bedroom, your leo will want to live somewhere else.

# Bringing your new leo home

A small ice chest works to bring your leo home from the store.

When you get home, gently release your leo into the tank.

Don't feed your gecko until the next day.

Leave him or her alone to explore and get used to their new home.

You should give them at least one week to get used to their tank before you pick them up.

Handle your leo as little as possible until they are at least 5 inches (almost 13 cm) long.

*Any leo would love to call this fancy vivarium his or her home!*

## Plants for Your Vivarium

Your pet will climb on plants in their tank. They might also try to eat them. For this reason, some pet owners use plastic plants. Live plants look better and the right kinds are safer for your leo. Never use silk plants. They have chemicals in them that aren't safe for pets.

Here are some plants that are safe for geckos. They're also strong, sturdy, easy to care for and they look good!

- Snake plant
- Pony-tail palm
- Philodendron

- Haworthia
- Climbing aloe
- Opuntia

All they need is the same amount of sunlight and warmth as your gecko needs. Water your vivarium plants once or twice a week.

### Leo Tip: Are leos picky eaters?

*Yes, they are. They only want to eat certain insects or insect worms. But they need to eat a variety of their favorite types of worms, just like wild leos do. They love crickets, but don't want to eat exactly the same thing for every meal!*

*Also, you might see reptile food flakes at your pet store and think that would make feeding easier.*

*Perhaps it would, for you. But not for your gecko. Unless their food is alive and moving, they won't want to eat it!*

### Leo Tip: How warm should the basking spot be?

*If you have only one or two leopard geckos in your vivarium, they need a basking spot big enough for two that is always 88 to 90 degrees F. (29 to 32 degrees C.)*

*If they are sharing their home with other types of lizards, the basking areas need to be 90 to 95 degrees F. (32 to 35 degrees C).*

# Chapter Five

# Good Care for Your Leo

Do this about two weeks after your new pet comes home.

At first, just put your hand down in the tank. Let your new pet get used to you slowly.

A curious leo who is ready to make friends will come over to your hand and might even climb onto it.

You will need to be patient with a baby or nervous gecko. It could take a month or longer for your gecko to feel comfortable being touched and ready to come out to visit with you.

*Like all pets, your leo needs time to get to know and trust you.*

# Be very, very gentle with your leo!

Never grab your leo or squeeze him or her.

Handle a leo like you would a brand new baby kitten or puppy.

Never pick him or her up by their tail.

Be really careful not to drop a pet leo!

Remember that loud noises or you moving suddenly frightens them.

You need to be calm and quiet when you are holding a gecko.

Don't be surprised if they poop on your hand.

Just put them back in their tank and wash your hands right away with soap and warm water.

One safe way to handle your gecko that both of you will enjoy is to let them crawl hand-over-hand when you sit on the floor, or on the couch.

# What could go wrong with your new pet?

Usually, very little can go wrong with a pet leo. They are easy to keep healthy and happy.

A leo that gets too fat needs to keep eating crickets but eat fewer superworms. Use superworms only for a treat, once a week.

Be careful not to let insect worms or crickets bite your leo. If your leo doesn't eat an insect or insect worm right away, don't leave the insect in the tank.

| If your leo is: | This could be the reason: |
|---|---|
| Weak, with swollen legs | They're not getting enough calcium. |
| Losing weight or has diarrhea | A bacterial infection. Go to the vet! |
| They are weak and thin. They might also be vomiting | A parasite infection. Go to the vet! |
| Having trouble shedding old skin from their toes | Be sure their wet hide is wet. Soak feet and very gently rub the old skin off |
| Lost their tail | Keep the wound clean. If infected, go to the vet. |

If you want to have two geckos, they must be females. Each gecko needs her own places to hide. Geckos do not want to share!

If you have two geckos, you need six hides. You also have to be sure that one gecko isn't taking all the food.

For two geckos to be comfortable and happy together, you might need a bigger tank. A vivarium that is 48 inches (122 cm) is ideal for two or a small group of geckos to share.

### Leo Tip: How to create a wet hide

*Your need one cool, damp hide where your leo can cool off. It also helps them at shedding time.*

*Your wet hide is just a regular hide, with moistened paper towel in it. Or you could put moistened foam sponge, vermiculite or sphagnum moss in their hide.*

# Stop! Don't kiss that lizard!

It is safe for you to have a lizard pet and handle it. It is NOT safe to kiss your lizard.

Don't do any of these things, because it's not safe:

1. Don't handle your pet and then touch your face.
2. Don't clean your pet's tank or <u>anything</u> from the tank in the kitchen sink or in the bathtub.
3. Don't forget to wear rubber gloves when cleaning the tank or anything in it.

To be safe, ALWAYS wash your hands carefully. Do this with warm water and soap before you handle your leo and also right after.

Keep your pet away from people food and where your family cooks your food.

This is important to help keep you and your leopard gecko healthy. Having a sick pet – or you or someone in your family being sick – is just no fun for anyone.

## More about substrate

You want the floor of your vivarium or tank to be comfortable for your leo's feet. It needs to not be something that could hurt them or make them sick.

Healthy substrate for babies or juveniles is newspaper or paper towel. The bad thing about these choices is that they don't look very nice. And you have to change them every couple of days.

By the time your pet is an adult, they want a substrate they can dig in. That is natural for a gecko. Shredded recycled paper is good for this. It should be about two inches (5 cm) deep. It is soft, absorbs waste and smells and looks good.

Or you could use cage carpet, also called reptile carpet. It comes in green or brown. Wash it every two weeks and cut off any hanging threads that could get caught in your pet's claws.

Play sand is another choice and it looks the most natural in a vivarium. You can buy it at toy, hardware and home improvement stores. It is also cheaper than reptile carpet. Sand is only a good choice for adults.

Slate, porcelain or ceramic tile, cut to fit your tank, is also an OK choice for substrate. Make sure there are no cracks between tiles that insects could hide in!

Every three months or so, when you do a total tank cleaning, throw out the old substrate, or clean the reptile carpet or tile with bleach-water or a white vinegar-water mix. Never use strong cleaning products meant for other pets, like cats or dogs.

## NEVER use these for substrate

Some of these choices are cheap or free. Or they are sold for some pet cages and are OK for other types of pets, but could be poisonous for a leopard gecko:

- Alfalfa pellets
- Calcium sand
- Shredded or whole corncobs
- Crushed walnut shells
- Coarse gravel
- Potting soil sold for growing houseplants
- Soil from outdoors

- Wood shavings
- Indoor/outdoor carpeting

## How warm does my leo want to be?

During the day the warm side of your tank should be between 84 to 88 degrees F. (or 29 to 31 degrees C.)

At night, the temperature shouldn't ever get colder than 65 degrees F. (18 degrees C.)

If your home is cooler than 70 degrees F. (21 degrees C.) at night, put an under-tank heater under the warm end of the tank. If you use this type of heater, the tank will need to be raised over the heater so some air can flow around the heater.

Keep your heaters on timers.

You will need to check that the temperatures are correct at least once a week. Measure everywhere in the vivarium that your pet can be. Use a thermometer with a probe or an infrared heat gun. You can find them online or for sale at reptile shows.

Do not use stick-on thermometers. They are almost never correct.

## About your tank lights

The easiest way to give a basking heat light to your pet is with an incandescent bulb. You put it in a clamp light fixture that has a reflector and place it at the top of the tank, at one end. The bulbs that go in it are

*A leo on a small glass globe.*

### *Leo Fact: Blue Leos?*

*All baby leos are born with bright blue or purple patches on top of their heads and between their eyes. This disappears by the time they are adults.*

ordinary 40-watt or 60-watt bulbs, the kind that go in table lamps.

Measure the temperature under the bulb at the spot where your leo can climb up and bask. It needs to be 84 to 88 degrees F. (29 to 31 degrees C.) in that spot.

Make sure that your heat light only heats up one end of the tank. Your leo needs to get away from the heat and cool off sometimes.

For light, you will need two full spectrum florescent bulbs that are about as long as the tank. They also hang at the top. One of these can be a UV light.

All your lights need to be on timers. These timers need to be set so your pet gets about 14 hours of 'daytime' light and warmth and 10 hours of dark sleep time every day.

## Does my pet need a UV light?

For many years, pet lizard breeders and owners have believed that leopard geckos are one of the types of lizards that don't need extra ultra-violet (UV) light. It seemed like their breeder animals and pets were doing just fine without it!

But recently, some breeders and owners have noticed that their leos seem happier and live longer when they do have a way to get their tails into some sunlight, as wild leopard geckos like to do.

It is difficult to get enough real sun for a pet leo, without putting their tank in direct sunlight, which can make their tank get way too hot. Pets have died from getting too hot and having no cooler place to go. They can't sweat and have no other way to cool their bodies. This is why they need a cool end of their tank and a cool hide.

The way for them to get light like the sun is to replace one of the regular florescent tube bulbs at the top of the tank with a UV bulb. There is no proof that you must do this for your pet's health. But it seems true to some experts. More research will give us an answer in the future!

If you do give your leo a UVB light, be sure they have hides when they want to get away from it. Also, if they have a UVB light, do NOT give them supplement Vitamin D. They'll get all they need from the light.

Lights should stay on for 14 hours a day except during the three winter months (or cooler months where you live). In winter, your pet might be brumating (that's lizard hibernation). If they are, they need shorter days. They might also need a 25-watt red light at night to give them just a little heat, but no light that could wake them up.

## Good Food For Leopard Geckos

Pet leos eat live crickets, roaches and insect worms. Adults can also have pinkie mice.

All the insects are sold in sizes from pinhead (very small) up, measured in how many inches (or centimeters) long they are.

Caring for a leo means also caring for their feeder insects, until they get eaten.

## Crickets or Locusts

Crickets (or locusts) are noisy. They chirp all the time. You might want to keep them in the basement or out in the garage, if it's warm enough. Otherwise all that chirping could be annoying!

They always need to be about 80 degrees F. (or 27 degrees C).

Keep them in a critter keeper. Or a plastic storage tub with breathing holes cut in it and mesh put over the holes or a screen top also works. It needs to be filled with pieces of egg cartons, to give them places to hide.

Feed your crickets or locusts slices of orange, sweet potato, carrot, apple or diced broccoli stem. You can put their food in a jar lid inside their enclosure.

You will need to empty out and clean your cricket box once every two weeks. Clean it the same way you do your leo's vivarium. To do this, it helps to have two cricket boxes, so they always live in one and the other one is always clean and ready for them to move to.

## Cockroaches

Cockroaches aren't welcome when they invade our homes! But they are a good, clean, nutritious food for leopard geckos!

A good home for them is an empty fish tank. It needs to be kept at about 85 degrees F. (29 degrees C.) all the time.

Feed them raw rolled oats and slices of bananas, apples, very ripe peaches or plums.

## Dubia Roaches

Another good leo food. They eat the same things as crickets, but live in their own critter cage.

## Phoenix Worms

These small white worms don't need to be fed. But they do need to stay cool, at about 60 degrees F. (16 degrees C.)

## Butter Worms

Butter worms are bright yellow. Keep them in the container they come in. They will do fine in the refrigerator until you give them to your leo.

## Tomato hornworms

Tomato hornworms are bright green. Keep them in the container they come in from the pet store (or buy them online). They are fine at normal room temperature.

## Waxworms

Waxworms are another type of white caterpillar. They are very high in fat, so only right for a special treat for your pet. They stay in the container they come in and must go in the refrigerator.

### Leo Tip: How much do pet leos eat?

*Young leos grow fast! To do that, they eat a lot! All leos eat 3 to 5 crickets or worms per meal.*

*Babies need to eat once or twice a day.*

*Juveniles have one meal a day or one meal every two days.*

*Adult leos have a meal two or three times a week.*

## What else does a leo need to eat?

To stay healthy, leos need extra calcium and Vitamin D3 (unless you have a UV light).

It's not easy to get these into your leo. You need to put some calcium carbonate in a small dish (a jar lid works) in their tank, and hope they decide to eat it.

But they might not. Here's what to do. Get these important supplements into your feeder insects. When your pet eats the insects, they also get their healthy supplements. Doing this is called gut-loading.

Feed insects with gut load about 24 hours before you feed the insects to your leo. You can buy powdered cricket food with beta carotene at the pet store made for this. Or here is how to make your own gut-load cricket food at home:

Put these into a blender:

- Dry flakes of baby food for people (one brand name is Pablum).
- Some calcium carbonate or calcium with D3 (if you don't have a UV light).

Mix and give to the crickets. Don't add any water!

Another way to gut-load is to put some of the same mixture in a bag. Add some crickets and shake the bag gently. The gut-load will stick to the crickets. Then feed them to your leo. This is faster and easier than feeding the mixture to the crickets first.

Juvenile leopard geckos need to get gut-loaded crickets or worms at every meal.

Adults get gut-loaded crickets two times a week.

*This is Tristan with his best lizard friend Gizmo. In this photo, Gizmo is about 6 months old.*

# Chapter Six

# What to Name Your Gecko

Are you wondering what to call your new pet? If so, here are some ideas.

You could give your gecko a 'people' name, like Molly or Sam.

You could find a name you like in your favourite movie or book. You might pick a name like Minion or Snape or Rango.

Maybe the name you like is from TV – names like Smurf, Muppet, or Geico.

Or it could just be a word you like – or even a word you make up!

## Here are some more names for your leo:

| Dragon | Bolt | Cookie |
|---|---|---|
| Princess | Widget | Sprout |
| Cuddles | Geek | Cupcake |
| Blondie | Burp | Squeaky |
| Bungee | Widget | Flash |
| Jujube | Gummy-Bear | Baby |
| Twinkle | Sprocket | Mr. Big |

## Leopard geckos can be a wonderful pet!

If you are interested in reptiles and excited about getting a leopard gecko, you will want to read lots more about them. This book has given you everything you need to know to get started.

We hope you have a happy time getting to know your new pet leopard gecko!

With good care, you and your leo could be best friends for many years to come!

Best wishes,

**Tristan and Jacquelyn**

## Got a question or comment?

Write to us here:

**Jacquelyn@CrimsonHillBooks.com**

# A Few Final Words

Well here we are. You've come to the last page and now we're asking you for a kind favour.

Would you be willing to submit an honest review about this book and your experience reading it? You might need an adult to help you do this.

Your review could help someone else decide to give it a try.

Of course, we hope for a positive review, but most important is an honest one.

So, if you could take a few moments to help us and anyone who might be considering reading this book, thanks so much.

And warm best wishes,

**Jackie, Wayne and Jesse**

The team at CrimsonHillBooks.com

Crimson Hill
Books

# Find all our books and our store at:

# www.CrimsonHillBooks.com

*Photo: Piotr Albanowicz, Pixabay.com*

## Gifts for Leopard Gecko Lovers!

Find phone covers, mugs and other fun gifts for leo lovers and everyone who likes pets when you visit:

## www.CrimsonHillBooks.com/Shop

# More Fun Books For Kids Who Love Pets!

**Best Pets for Kids series:**

I Want A Leopard Gecko

I Want A Bearded Dragon

I Want A Puppy Or A Dog

I Want A Kitten Or A Cat

**Fun Animal Facts for Kids series:**

Fun Dog Facts For Kids 9-12

Fun Cat Facts For Kids 9-12

Fun Leopard Gecko and Bearded Dragon Facts For Kids 9-12

Fun Reptile Facts For Kids 9-12

**Fun Pets for Kids series:**

Small Fun Pets: Beginning Pets For Kids 9-12

Top 10 Fun Pets for Kids 9-12

## Find them all at:
## www.CrimsonHillBooks.com

Made in the USA
Monee, IL
15 December 2020

53476010R00040